Freelance Writer's Work Order Logbook

for the dates of

__________________________*through*__________________________

Introduction

People have sought ways to make money from home for decades. Before the advent of the Internet, that meant taking in laundry or somebody else's children. With the dawning of the information age, ads for "Work From Home" opportunities flooded our world with the vast majority being little more than a scam.

Today, the world is fast becoming a global gig economy with freelance writing being one of the most legitimate home work opportunities out there. There are a number of legitimate platforms through which freelance writers can find work including WriterAccess, Crowd Content and Textbroker.

Once you've taken the leap and found platforms to work through, the next thing to do is get organized. That is where this book comes in handy. Chances are, you'll be working for a number of different clients who each have their own idea of what good content looks like with questions that include:

- Should you use the Oxford comma?
- Which point of view should the copy be written in?
- Who is the target audience?
- What tone should the piece take?
- When is it due?

This book provides content order forms which can be filled out with as little or as much information as you choose. It helps you keep all the information you need for each assignment in one place that can be referred to as you write.

Never forget to include or exclude an Oxford — aka serial — comma again. Have that list of keywords you need to include right there to check off. Use the order to check off necessary elements as you proofread your work. Keep track of those deadlines so you don't miss them.

The last five pages contain accounting forms to help keep track of the time spent on and payment received for each assignment. Once you've filled the book with your work as a freelance writer, you can save it for the financial records of your new business.

However you use this book, the most important thing you can do for your career as a freelance writer is to WRITE ON!!!

ORDER #	$
Client:	

Word Count: _______ to _______   Oxford Comma

Point of View: 1st   2nd   3rd

Tone: _______________________________

Audience: ____________________________

Keyword(s):		

NOTES:
____
____
____
____
____
____
____
____
____
____
____
____
____
____
____
____

Due:	Submitted:	Revised:

ORDER #	$
Client:	

Word Count: _____________ to _____________   Oxford Comma

Point of View: 1st   2nd   3rd

Tone: _______________________________

Audience: ___________________________

Keyword(s):		

NOTES:

Due:		Submitted:		Revised:	

ORDER #		$
Client:		

Word Count: _______________ to _______________   Oxford Comma

Point of View: 1ˢᵗ   2ⁿᵈ   3ʳᵈ

Tone: ____

Audience: ____

Keyword(s):		

NOTES: ____

____

____

____

____

____

____

____

____

____

____

____

____

____

____

____

Due:		Submitted:		Revised:	

ORDER #		$
Client:		

Word Count: _____________ to _____________ Oxford Comma

Point of View: 1st 2nd 3rd

Tone: _______________________________________

Audience: ____________________________________

Keyword(s):				

NOTES:

____
____
____
____
____
____
____
____
____
____
____
____
____
____
____
____
____

Due:		Submitted:		Revised:	

ORDER #		$
Client:		

Word Count: ___________ to ___________   Oxford Comma

Point of View: 1st   2nd   3rd

Tone: ___________________________________

Audience: ________________________________

Keyword(s):		

NOTES: ___________________________________

____

____

____

____

____

____

____

____

____

____

____

____

____

____

____

____

____

Due:		Submitted:		Revised:	

ORDER #	$
Client:	

Word Count: _______ to _______   Oxford Comma

Point of View: 1st   2nd   3rd

Tone: ______________________________

Audience: ____________________________

Keyword(s):		

NOTES:

Due:		Submitted:		Revised:	

ORDER #	$
Client:	

Word Count: _____________ to _____________   Oxford Comma

Point of View: 1st   2nd   3rd

Tone: _______________________________________

Audience: ___________________________________

Keyword(s):		

NOTES: ______________________________________

____

____

____

____

____

____

____

____

____

____

____

____

____

____

____

____

Due:	Submitted:	Revised:

<table>
<tr><td>ORDER #</td><td>$</td></tr>
<tr><td>Client:</td><td></td></tr>
</table>

Word Count: _______ to _______   Oxford Comma

Point of View: 1st   2nd   3rd

Tone: _______________________________

Audience: _______________________________

<table>
<tr><td rowspan="5">Keyword(s):</td><td></td><td></td></tr>
<tr><td></td><td></td></tr>
<tr><td></td><td></td></tr>
<tr><td></td><td></td></tr>
<tr><td></td><td></td></tr>
</table>

NOTES:

<table>
<tr><td>Due:</td><td></td><td>Submitted:</td><td></td><td>Revised:</td><td></td></tr>
</table>

ORDER #		$
Client:		

Word Count: _________________ to _________________ Oxford Comma

Point of View: 1st 2nd 3rd

Tone: ____

Audience: ____

Keyword(s):		

NOTES: ____

Due:		Submitted:		Revised:	

ORDER #	$
Client:	

Word Count: _____________ to _____________   Oxford Comma

Point of View: 1st   2nd   3rd

Tone: _______________________________

Audience: ____________________________

Keyword(s):		

NOTES:
____
____
____
____
____
____
____
____
____
____
____
____
____
____
____
____
____

Due:		Submitted:		Revised:	

ORDER #		$
Client:		

Word Count: _______________ to _______________   Oxford Comma

Point of View: 1st   2nd   3rd

Tone: ____

Audience: ____

Keyword(s):		

NOTES: ____

____

____

____

____

____

____

____

____

____

____

____

____

____

____

____

Due:		Submitted:		Revised:	

ORDER #		$
Client:		

Word Count: _______ to _______ Oxford Comma

Point of View: 1st 2nd 3rd

Tone: _______

Audience: _______

Keyword(s):		

NOTES:

Due:		Submitted:		Revised:	

ORDER #	$
Client:	

Word Count: _______________ to _______________   Oxford Comma

Point of View: 1st   2nd   3rd

Tone: ____

Audience: ____

Keyword(s):		

NOTES:

____
____
____
____
____
____
____
____
____
____
____
____
____
____
____
____
____
____

Due:		Submitted:		Revised:	

<table>
<tr><td>ORDER #</td><td>$</td></tr>
<tr><td>Client:</td><td></td></tr>
</table>

Word Count: _______ to _______   Oxford Comma

Point of View: 1st   2nd   3rd

Tone: _________________________________

Audience: _________________________________

Keyword(s):		

NOTES:
____
____
____
____
____
____
____
____
____
____
____
____
____
____
____
____
____

Due:		Submitted:		Revised:	

ORDER #	$
Client:	

Word Count: _______________ to _______________   Oxford Comma

Point of View: 1st   2nd   3rd

Tone: ____

Audience: ____

Keyword(s):		

NOTES: ____

Due:		Submitted:		Revised:	

ORDER #		$
Client:		

Word Count: _____________ to _____________   Oxford Comma

Point of View: 1st   2nd   3rd

Tone: _______________________________

Audience: _______________________________

Keyword(s):		

NOTES:

____
____
____
____
____
____
____
____
____
____
____
____
____
____
____
____
____

Due:		Submitted:		Revised:	

<table>
<tr><td>ORDER #</td><td></td><td>$</td></tr>
<tr><td>Client:</td><td></td><td></td></tr>
</table>

Word Count: ________________ to ________________ Oxford Comma

Point of View: 1ˢᵗ 2ⁿᵈ 3ʳᵈ

Tone: ________________________________

Audience: ________________________________

<table>
<tr><td rowspan="5">Keyword(s):</td><td></td><td></td></tr>
<tr><td></td><td></td></tr>
<tr><td></td><td></td></tr>
<tr><td></td><td></td></tr>
<tr><td></td><td></td></tr>
</table>

NOTES: ________________________________

____

____

____

____

____

____

____

____

____

____

____

____

____

____

____

____

____

<table>
<tr><td>Due:</td><td></td><td>Submitted:</td><td></td><td>Revised:</td><td></td></tr>
</table>

ORDER #		$
Client:		

Word Count: _____________ to _____________   Oxford Comma

Point of View: 1st   2nd   3rd

Tone: _______________________________________

Audience: ____________________________________

Keyword(s):		

NOTES:
____
____
____
____
____
____
____
____
____
____
____
____
____
____
____

Due:		Submitted:		Revised:	

ORDER #		$
Client:		

Word Count: _______________ to _______________   Oxford Comma

Point of View: 1st   2nd   3rd

Tone: ____

Audience: ____

Keyword(s):		

NOTES: ____
____
____
____
____
____
____
____
____
____
____
____
____
____
____
____
____

Due:		Submitted:		Revised:	

ORDER #	$
Client:	

Word Count: _____________ to _____________   Oxford Comma

Point of View: 1st   2nd   3rd

Tone: _____________________________________

Audience: _________________________________

Keyword(s):		

NOTES:
____
____
____
____
____
____
____
____
____
____
____
____
____
____
____
____
____
____

Due:		Submitted:		Revised:	

ORDER #		$
Client:		

Word Count: _______________ to _______________   Oxford Comma

Point of View: 1st   2nd   3rd

Tone: _______________________________________

Audience: ___________________________________

Keyword(s):		

NOTES: _______________________________________

____

____

____

____

____

____

____

____

____

____

____

____

____

____

____

____

Due:		Submitted:		Revised:	

ORDER #		$
Client:		

Word Count: ______________ to ______________   Oxford Comma

Point of View: 1st   2nd   3rd

Tone: ____

Audience: ____

Keyword(s):		

NOTES:

____

____

____

____

____

____

____

____

____

____

____

____

____

____

____

____

____

Due:		Submitted:		Revised:	

ORDER #		$
Client:		

Word Count: ___________ to ___________   Oxford Comma

Point of View: 1st   2nd   3rd

Tone: ___________________________________

Audience: _______________________________

Keyword(s):		

NOTES: ___________________________________

Due:		Submitted:		Revised:	

ORDER #	$
Client:	

Word Count: _____________ to _____________ Oxford Comma

Point of View: 1st 2nd 3rd

Tone: _______________________________________

Audience: ____________________________________

Keyword(s):		

NOTES:

Due:		Submitted:		Revised:	

ORDER #	$
Client:	

Word Count: ______________ to ______________   Oxford Comma

Point of View: 1st   2nd   3rd

Tone: ____

Audience: ____

Keyword(s):		

NOTES:
____
____
____
____
____
____
____
____
____
____
____
____
____
____
____
____
____
____

Due:		Submitted:		Revised:	

ORDER #		$

Client:

Word Count: _______________ to _______________ Oxford Comma

Point of View: 1st   2nd   3rd

Tone: _______________________________________

Audience: ____________________________________

Keyword(s):		

NOTES:

____
____
____
____
____
____
____
____
____
____
____
____
____
____
____
____

Due:		Submitted:		Revised:	

ORDER #		$

Client:

Word Count: _____________ to _____________   Oxford Comma

Point of View: 1st   2nd   3rd

Tone: ____

Audience: ____

Keyword(s):		

NOTES: ____

____

____

____

____

____

____

____

____

____

____

____

____

____

____

____

____

____

____

Due:		Submitted:		Revised:	

ORDER #	$
Client:	

Word Count: _______________ to _______________   Oxford Comma

Point of View: 1st   2nd   3rd

Tone: _______________

Audience: _______________

Keyword(s):		

NOTES:
____
____
____
____
____
____
____
____
____
____
____
____
____
____
____
____

Due:		Submitted:		Revised:	

ORDER #	$
Client:	

Word Count: _______________ to _______________   Oxford Comma

Point of View: 1st   2nd   3rd

Tone: _______________

Audience: _______________

Keyword(s):		

NOTES:

| Due: | | Submitted: | | Revised: | |

ORDER #	$
Client:	

Word Count: _____________ to _____________ Oxford Comma

Point of View: 1st 2nd 3rd

Tone: _____________________________________

Audience: _________________________________

Keyword(s):		

NOTES:

____
____
____
____
____
____
____
____
____
____
____
____
____
____
____
____
____

Due:		Submitted:		Revised:	

ORDER #	$
Client:	

Word Count: _________________ to _________________   Oxford Comma

Point of View: 1st   2nd   3rd

Tone: ____

Audience: ____

Keyword(s):		

NOTES: ____

____

____

____

____

____

____

____

____

____

____

____

____

____

____

____

____

____

Due:		Submitted:		Revised:	

ORDER #	$
Client:	

Word Count: ___________ to ___________   Oxford Comma

Point of View: 1st   2nd   3rd

Tone: _______________________________________

Audience: ____________________________________

Keyword(s):		

NOTES: ____

____

____

____

____

____

____

____

____

____

____

____

____

____

____

____

____

____

Due:		Submitted:		Revised:	

ORDER #		$	
Client:			

Word Count: _________ to _________   Oxford Comma

Point of View: 1st   2nd   3rd

Tone: ____

Audience: ____

Keyword(s):		

NOTES: ____

____

____

____

____

____

____

____

____

____

____

____

____

____

____

____

____

____

____

Due:		Submitted:		Revised:	

ORDER #		$	
Client:			

Word Count: ___________ to ___________ Oxford Comma

Point of View: 1st 2nd 3rd

Tone: ____

Audience: _______________________________________

Keyword(s):		

NOTES:
____
____
____
____
____
____
____
____
____
____
____
____
____
____
____

Due:		Submitted:		Revised:	

ORDER #		$
Client:		

Word Count: _____________ to _____________   Oxford Comma

Point of View: 1st   2nd   3rd

Tone: ____

Audience: ____

Keyword(s):		

NOTES: ____

____

____

____

____

____

____

____

____

____

____

____

____

____

____

____

____

Due:		Submitted:		Revised:	

<table>
<tr><td>ORDER #</td><td>$</td></tr>
<tr><td>Client:</td><td></td></tr>
</table>

Word Count: _______ to _______   Oxford Comma

Point of View: 1st   2nd   3rd

Tone: _______________________________

Audience: ___________________________

Keyword(s):		

NOTES: _______________________________

____

____

____

____

____

____

____

____

____

____

____

____

____

____

____

____

Due:		Submitted:		Revised:	

ORDER #	$
Client:	

Word Count: _____________ to _____________ Oxford Comma

Point of View: 1st   2nd   3rd

Tone: _______________________________

Audience: _______________________________

Keyword(s):		

NOTES:

Due:		Submitted:		Revised:	

ORDER #	$
Client:	

Word Count: _______________ to _______________   Oxford Comma

Point of View: 1st   2nd   3rd

Tone: ____

Audience: ____

Keyword(s):		

NOTES: ____

____
____
____
____
____
____
____
____
____
____
____
____
____
____

Due:		Submitted:		Revised:	

ORDER #	$
Client:	

Word Count: __________ to __________   Oxford Comma

Point of View: 1st   2nd   3rd

Tone: ____________________________

Audience: ____________________________

Keyword(s):		

NOTES:
____
____
____
____
____
____
____
____
____
____
____
____
____
____
____
____
____

Due:		Submitted:		Revised:	

<table>
<tr><td>ORDER #</td><td>$</td></tr>
<tr><td>Client:</td><td></td></tr>
</table>

Word Count: _____ to _____   Oxford Comma

Point of View: 1st   2nd   3rd

Tone: _____________________

Audience: _____________________

Keyword(s):		

NOTES:

____
____
____
____
____
____
____
____
____
____
____
____
____
____
____
____
____

Due:		Submitted:		Revised:	

ORDER #		$
Client:		

Word Count: _______________ to _______________ Oxford Comma

Point of View: 1st   2nd   3rd

Tone: _______________________________________

Audience: ____________________________________

Keyword(s):		

NOTES:

____

____

____

____

____

____

____

____

____

____

____

____

____

____

____

____

____

Due:		Submitted:		Revised:	

ORDER #	$

Client:

Word Count: _______________ to _______________   Oxford Comma

Point of View: 1st   2nd   3rd

Tone: _______________________________________

Audience: ___________________________________

Keyword(s):		

NOTES:

Due:		Submitted:		Revised:	

ORDER #	$
Client:	

Word Count: __________ to __________   Oxford Comma

Point of View: 1st   2nd   3rd

Tone: __________________________________

Audience: ______________________________

Keyword(s):		

NOTES:
____
____
____
____
____
____
____
____
____
____
____
____
____
____
____
____

Due:		Submitted:		Revised:	

ORDER #	$
Client:	

Word Count: _______________ to _______________   Oxford Comma

Point of View: 1st   2nd   3rd

Tone: ____

Audience: ____

Keyword(s):		

NOTES:

Due:		Submitted:		Revised:	

ORDER #	$
Client:	

Word Count: ______________ to ______________   Oxford Comma

Point of View: 1st   2nd   3rd

Tone: ____

Audience: ____

Keyword(s):		

NOTES: ____

____

____

____

____

____

____

____

____

____

____

____

____

____

____

Due:		Submitted:		Revised:	

ORDER #		$
Client:		

Word Count: _______________ to _______________   Oxford Comma

Point of View: 1st   2nd   3rd

Tone: _______________________________________

Audience: _______________________________________

Keyword(s):		

NOTES:

____

____

____

____

____

____

____

____

____

____

____

____

____

____

____

Due:		Submitted:		Revised:	

ORDER #		$
Client:		

Word Count: _________________ to _________________   Oxford Comma

Point of View: 1st   2nd   3rd

Tone: ____

Audience: ____

Keyword(s):		

NOTES: ____

____

____

____

____

____

____

____

____

____

____

____

____

____

____

____

____

Due:		Submitted:		Revised:	

ORDER #	$
Client:	

Word Count: _____________ to _____________ Oxford Comma

Point of View: 1st   2nd   3rd

Tone: ____

Audience: ____

Keyword(s):		

NOTES:
____
____
____
____
____
____
____
____
____
____
____
____
____
____
____
____

Due:		Submitted:		Revised:	

ORDER #	$
Client:	

Word Count: _____________ to _____________   Oxford Comma

Point of View: 1st   2nd   3rd

Tone: _______________________________________

Audience: ___________________________________

Keyword(s):		

NOTES:

Due:		Submitted:		Revised:	

<table>
<tr><td>ORDER #</td><td>$</td></tr>
<tr><td>Client:</td><td></td></tr>
</table>

Word Count: _____________ to _____________   Oxford Comma

Point of View: 1st   2nd   3rd

Tone: _______________________________________

Audience: ___________________________________

Keyword(s):		

NOTES:
____
____
____
____
____
____
____
____
____
____
____
____
____
____
____
____
____

Due:		Submitted:		Revised:	

ORDER #	$
Client:	

Word Count: _____________ to _____________   Oxford Comma

Point of View: 1st   2nd   3rd

Tone: _____________________________________

Audience: _________________________________

Keyword(s):		

NOTES:

Due:		Submitted:		Revised:	

ORDER #		$	
Client:			

Word Count: _______________ to _______________ Oxford Comma

Point of View: 1st   2nd   3rd

Tone: ____

Audience: ____

Keyword(s):		

NOTES:
____
____
____
____
____
____
____
____
____
____
____
____
____
____
____
____
____

Due:		Submitted:		Revised:	

ORDER #		$
Client:		

Word Count: _____________ to _____________ Oxford Comma

Point of View: 1st 2nd 3rd

Tone: ____

Audience: ______________________________________

Keyword(s):		

NOTES: ____

Due:		Submitted:		Revised:	

ORDER #	$
Client:	

Word Count: __________ to __________ Oxford Comma

Point of View: 1st   2nd   3rd

Tone: ________________________________

Audience: ___________________________

Keyword(s):		

NOTES:

Due:		Submitted:		Revised:	

<table>
<tr><td>ORDER #</td><td rowspan="2">$</td></tr>
<tr><td>Client:</td></tr>
</table>

Word Count: ______________ to ______________   Oxford Comma

Point of View: 1st   2nd   3rd

Tone: _______________________________________

Audience: ___________________________________

<table>
<tr><td rowspan="4">Keyword(s):</td><td></td><td></td></tr>
<tr><td></td><td></td></tr>
<tr><td></td><td></td></tr>
<tr><td></td><td></td></tr>
</table>

NOTES:

Due:		Submitted:		Revised:	

ORDER #	$
Client:	

Word Count: ______________ to ______________ Oxford Comma

Point of View: 1st 2nd 3rd

Tone: ____

Audience: ____

Keyword(s):		

NOTES:

____
____
____
____
____
____
____
____
____
____
____
____
____
____
____
____
____
____

Due:		Submitted:		Revised:	

ORDER #	$
Client:	

Word Count: ______________ to ______________   Oxford Comma

Point of View: 1st   2nd   3rd

Tone: ____

Audience: ____

Keyword(s):		

NOTES:

____

____

____

____

____

____

____

____

____

____

____

____

____

____

____

____

____

Due:		Submitted:		Revised:	

ORDER #		$
Client:		

Word Count: _______________ to _______________ Oxford Comma

Point of View: 1st   2nd   3rd

Tone: _______________________________________

Audience: ___________________________________

Keyword(s):		

NOTES:

Due:		Submitted:		Revised:	

<table>
<tr><td>ORDER #</td><td>$</td></tr>
<tr><td>Client:</td><td></td></tr>
</table>

Word Count: _____________ to _____________ Oxford Comma

Point of View: 1st 2nd 3rd

Tone: _______________________________________

Audience: ___________________________________

Keyword(s):		

NOTES: _______________________________________

____

____

____

____

____

____

____

____

____

____

____

____

____

____

____

____

Due:		Submitted:		Revised:	

ORDER #	$
Client:	

Word Count: _______________ to _______________   Oxford Comma

Point of View: 1st   2nd   3rd

Tone: ____

Audience: ____

Keyword(s):		

NOTES:
____
____
____
____
____
____
____
____
____
____
____
____
____
____
____
____
____
____

Due:		Submitted:		Revised:	

ORDER #		$	
Client:			

Word Count: _______________ to _______________   Oxford Comma

Point of View: 1ˢᵗ   2ⁿᵈ   3ʳᵈ

Tone: ____

Audience: ____

Keyword(s):		

NOTES: ____

____

____

____

____

____

____

____

____

____

____

____

____

____

____

____

____

Due:		Submitted:		Revised:	

<table>
<tr><td>ORDER #</td><td>$</td></tr>
</table>

Client:

Word Count: _______ to _______   Oxford Comma

Point of View: 1st   2nd   3rd

Tone: _______________________

Audience: _______________________

Keyword(s):

NOTES:

Due: Submitted: Revised:

ORDER #	$
Client:	

Word Count: _______________ to _______________   Oxford Comma

Point of View: 1st   2nd   3rd

Tone: ____

Audience: ____

Keyword(s):		

NOTES:

Due:		Submitted:		Revised:	

ORDER #	$
Client:	

Word Count: __________ to __________   Oxford Comma

Point of View: 1st   2nd   3rd

Tone: ______________________________

Audience: ______________________________

Keyword(s):		

NOTES:
____
____
____
____
____
____
____
____
____
____
____
____
____
____
____
____
____

Due:		Submitted:		Revised:	

ORDER #		$	
Client:			

Word Count: _______________ to _______________   Oxford Comma

Point of View: 1st   2nd   3rd

Tone: ____

Audience: ____

Keyword(s):		

NOTES: ____

____

____

____

____

____

____

____

____

____

____

____

____

____

____

____

____

____

Due:		Submitted:		Revised:	

ORDER #	$
Client:	

Word Count: _______________ to _______________   Oxford Comma

Point of View: 1st 2nd 3rd

Tone: _______________________________________

Audience: ____________________________________

Keyword(s):		

NOTES:

____
____
____
____
____
____
____
____
____
____
____
____
____
____
____
____
____

Due:		Submitted:		Revised:	

<table>
<tr><td>ORDER #</td><td>$</td></tr>
<tr><td>Client:</td><td></td></tr>
</table>

Word Count: _____________ to _____________   Oxford Comma

Point of View: 1st   2nd   3rd

Tone: _____________________________________

Audience: _________________________________

Keyword(s):		

NOTES: _____________________________________

____

____

____

____

____

____

____

____

____

____

____

____

____

____

____

____

Due:		Submitted:		Revised:	

ORDER #	$
Client:	

Word Count: _____________ to _____________ Oxford Comma

Point of View: 1st   2nd   3rd

Tone: _______________________________________

Audience: ___________________________________

Keyword(s):		

NOTES:
____
____
____
____
____
____
____
____
____
____
____
____
____
____
____
____
____

Due:	Submitted:	Revised:

ORDER #		$	
Client:			

Word Count: _______________ to _______________   Oxford Comma

Point of View: 1st   2nd   3rd

Tone: _______________________________________

Audience: _______________________________________

Keyword(s):		

NOTES:

Due:		Submitted:		Revised:	

ORDER #	$
Client:	

Word Count: ___________ to ___________ Oxford Comma

Point of View: 1st 2nd 3rd

Tone: _______________________

Audience: _______________________

Keyword(s):		

NOTES:

Due:		Submitted:		Revised:	

ORDER #	$
Client:	

Word Count: _________________ to _________________   Oxford Comma

Point of View: 1st   2nd   3rd

Tone: ____

Audience: ____

Keyword(s):		

NOTES: ____

____

____

____

____

____

____

____

____

____

____

____

____

____

____

____

Due:		Submitted:		Revised:	

ORDER #	$
Client:	

Word Count: _____________ to _____________   Oxford Comma

Point of View: 1st   2nd   3rd

Tone: _______________________________________

Audience: ___________________________________

Keyword(s):		

NOTES:

Due:	Submitted:	Revised:

ORDER #		$	
Client:			

Word Count: ________________ to ________________   Oxford Comma

Point of View: 1st   2nd   3rd

Tone: ____

Audience: ____

Keyword(s):		

NOTES:
____
____
____
____
____
____
____
____
____
____
____
____
____
____
____
____
____
____
____
____

Due:		Submitted:		Revised:	

ORDER #	$
Client:	

Word Count: ______________ to ______________   Oxford Comma

Point of View: 1st   2nd   3rd

Tone: ____

Audience: ____

Keyword(s):		

NOTES:
____
____
____
____
____
____
____
____
____
____
____
____
____
____
____
____
____

Due:		Submitted:		Revised:	

ORDER #	$

Client:

Word Count: __________ to __________   Oxford Comma

Point of View: 1st   2nd   3rd

Tone: ____

Audience: ______________________________________

Keyword(s):		

NOTES: ____

____

____

____

____

____

____

____

____

____

____

____

____

____

____

____

____

Due:		Submitted:		Revised:	

<table>
<tr><td>ORDER #</td><td rowspan="2">$</td></tr>
<tr><td>Client:</td></tr>
</table>

Word Count: _______________ to _______________   Oxford Comma

Point of View: 1st   2nd   3rd

Tone: ____

Audience: ____

Keyword(s):		

NOTES: ____
____
____
____
____
____
____
____
____
____
____
____
____
____
____
____
____
____
____

Due:		Submitted:		Revised:	

ORDER #		$
Client:		

Word Count: _______ to _______ Oxford Comma

Point of View: 1st 2nd 3rd

Tone: _______________________

Audience: _______________________

Keyword(s):		

NOTES:

Due:		Submitted:		Revised:	

ORDER #	$
Client:	

Word Count: _______ to _______   Oxford Comma

Point of View: 1st   2nd   3rd

Tone: _______________________________

Audience: _______________________________

Keyword(s):		

NOTES: _______________________________

____

____

____

____

____

____

____

____

____

____

____

____

____

____

____

Due:		Submitted:		Revised:	

ORDER #	$
Client:	

Word Count: _____________ to _____________ Oxford Comma

Point of View: 1st   2nd   3rd

Tone: _______________________________

Audience: _______________________________

Keyword(s):		

NOTES:

____

____

____

____

____

____

____

____

____

____

____

____

____

____

____

____

Due:		Submitted:		Revised:	

ORDER #		$	
Client:			

Word Count: __________ to __________   Oxford Comma

Point of View: 1st   2nd   3rd

Tone: ______________________________

Audience: ____________________________

Keyword(s):		

NOTES:

____
____
____
____
____
____
____
____
____
____
____
____
____
____
____
____
____
____

Due:		Submitted:		Revised:	

ORDER #		$	
Client:			

Word Count: _______________ to _______________   Oxford Comma

Point of View: 1st   2nd   3rd

Tone: ____

Audience: ____

Keyword(s):		

NOTES: ____
____
____
____
____
____
____
____
____
____
____
____
____
____
____
____
____
____

Due:		Submitted:		Revised:	

ORDER #	$
Client:	

Word Count: ________________ to ________________   Oxford Comma

Point of View: 1st   2nd   3rd

Tone: ____

Audience: ____

Keyword(s):		

NOTES:
____
____
____
____
____
____
____
____
____
____
____
____
____
____
____
____
____

Due:		Submitted:		Revised:	

ORDER #	$
Client:	

Word Count: _________ to _________   Oxford Comma

Point of View: 1st   2nd   3rd

Tone: _______________________________

Audience: _______________________________

Keyword(s):		

NOTES: _______________________________

____

____

____

____

____

____

____

____

____

____

____

____

____

____

____

____

____

Due:		Submitted:		Revised:	

ORDER #		$
Client:		

Word Count: _______________ to _______________   Oxford Comma

Point of View: 1st   2nd   3rd

Tone: ____

Audience: ____

Keyword(s):		

NOTES: ____

____

____

____

____

____

____

____

____

____

____

____

____

____

____

____

____

Due:		Submitted:		Revised:	

ORDER #	$
Client:	

Word Count: ___________ to ___________   Oxford Comma

Point of View: 1st   2nd   3rd

Tone: _______________________________________

Audience: ___________________________________

Keyword(s):		

NOTES:
____
____
____
____
____
____
____
____
____
____
____
____
____
____
____
____
____
____

Due:		Submitted:		Revised:	

ORDER #		$
Client:		

Word Count: _____________ to _____________ Oxford Comma

Point of View: 1st 2nd 3rd

Tone: _______________________________

Audience: _______________________________

Keyword(s):		

NOTES:

Due:		Submitted:		Revised:	

ORDER #		$
Client:		

Word Count: _______________ to _______________   Oxford Comma

Point of View: 1st   2nd   3rd

Tone: ____

Audience: ____

Keyword(s):		

NOTES: ____

____

____

____

____

____

____

____

____

____

____

____

____

____

____

____

____

____

Due:		Submitted:		Revised:	

ORDER #	$
Client:	

Word Count: _______________ to _______________   Oxford Comma

Point of View: 1st   2nd   3rd

Tone: ____

Audience: ____

Keyword(s):		

NOTES:
____
____
____
____
____
____
____
____
____
____
____
____
____
____
____
____
____

Due:		Submitted:		Revised:	

ORDER #		$	
Client:			

Word Count: ____________ to ____________   Oxford Comma

Point of View: 1st   2nd   3rd

Tone: ________________________________

Audience: ________________________________

Keyword(s):		

NOTES: ________________________________
____
____
____
____
____
____
____
____
____
____
____
____
____
____
____
____
____
____

Due:		Submitted:		Revised:	

ORDER #	$
Client:	

Word Count: ______________ to ______________   Oxford Comma

Point of View: 1st   2nd   3rd

Tone: ___________________________________

Audience: ________________________________

Keyword(s):		

NOTES: ___________________________________
____
____
____
____
____
____
____
____
____
____
____
____
____
____
____
____

Due:		Submitted:		Revised:	

ORDER #	WORDS	TIME	$	ACCEPTED	PAID
ORDER #	WORDS	TIME	$	ACCEPTED	PAID

ORDER #	WORDS	TIME	$	ACCEPTED	PAID

ORDER #	WORDS	TIME	$	ACCEPTED	PAID

ORDER #	WORDS	TIME	$	ACCEPTED	PAID
ORDER #	WORDS	TIME	$	ACCEPTED	PAID

ORDER #	WORDS	TIME	$	ACCEPTED	PAID

ORDER #	WORDS	TIME	$	ACCEPTED	PAID

ORDER #	WORDS	TIME	$	ACCEPTED	PAID
ORDER #	WORDS	TIME	$	ACCEPTED	PAID